THE
GOLDEN BOOK
OF POEMS

— • —

HERMAN F GAPOUR

AuthorHouse™
1663 Liberty Drive
Bloomington, IN 47403
www.authorhouse.com
Phone: 1 (800) 839-8640

Published by AuthorHouse 04/30/2019

ISBN: 978-1-5462-7363-9 (sc)
ISBN: 978-1-7283-1053-4 (hc)
ISBN: 978-1-5462-7364-6 (e)

Library of Congress Control Number: 2018915254

Print information available on the last page.

This book is printed on acid-free paper.

authorHOUSE®

About the Book

This book is based on the Life and Love of Humanity. Love that was there when we were children, but somewhere along this road of life we lost that love and respect for each others. Many times I ask myself the question why? And you too can also ask yourself the same question why? Imagine yourself as the only human being on this wonderful planet, where would you go? What would you do? Would there be love in your heart, or would you say to yourself what is my reason for living.

For a life without love is a life without hope of being the person that you wanted to be. And as we live to see another day we try to eliminate that little love from our daily lives and forget about that love of yesterday. So let us teach our children the love from our hearts and from our childhood past. And when we have done it that will live in them for the rest of their lives. And will make this world a better place for us to live. So while we are here let us show love and be happy rather than the opposite side of love.

Let us searched our hearts and our minds and try to find where we lost the love that was there, so that we can make it real again and to exercise that love once more, for the love and dignity of all. Whether we are great or whether we are small, love makes the world go around. Only love can conquer it all.

CONTENTS

THE
GOLDEN BOOK
OF POEMS

LOVE AND HATE

We are lost like a needle in a haystack, lost without hope and being unable to find who we are and what we are. The mentality of men is so corrupt, that I will see you fall and I will never pick you up because I have no love inside of me so how can I show you what love is when I do not know what love is so as I look upon you I can despise you whether you are guilty or not and I can condemn you like the leaves that fall from the branches of a tree and care not as I pass you by. We must remember life is short but we take it for granted so let us share the love that is in us today and tomorrow will tell for itself as we face another day in a life that is given to us but does not belong to us.

I Am Only Human

Blame me not for what you have done but respect me for what I am. In the eyes I see a human being with a mind of their own yet day after day you are what you are but look into yourself and see what is wrong and try to mend it as you go along. The chance we have today can only eliminate from our lives tomorrow. As we live among the ones that hate and hate without a cause the ones that love and love with all their hearts. Let us not judge so that we can be judged but to live as a human being with love respect and integrity for it will not only live within us but will also live within our children and our children's children in the years to come .

FAITH AND PEACE

I was tormented with many obstacles during my life but I managed to overcome them as I live from day to day, not by sight but by the faith that I strongly believed in. It is not easy to accept obstacles as we live day by day but everything has an end, even the greatest of storms or the mightiest of winds will come to an end because nothing is here forever. I have lost track of many things in my life but I will never lose track of the hate I have been through in this life that I have lived. I have been talked down and ridiculed, persecuted and even condemn but I will not let my fears conquer my faith because one minute in life is worth more than a thousand years without life, and as I live I will live by faith and not by sight. I will live with love, I will live with harmony but most of all I will try to accomplish peace with humanity and everything that is around me.

THE JOURNEY OF LIFE

As I stare at the horizon that is far and beyond, it is telling me of something that I do not know. I have learned some of what is there to know but there is so much more that I do not know but the longer I live I will try to achieve more only if I want to know more. The days of our lives are numbered as we go along and to everything this is a song that we ought to know. Let us not forget where we came from but be thankful of what we are, and as we live to see one day and hoping to see another day, I am pleading to all mankind let there be love, respect and be of a kind heart, not only to your brothers and sisters but to a human being just like yourself, let my pain be your pain and your grief be my grief. There and then we will have love peace and prosperity and not a human race that divided themselves against each other, but as a human being to another human being as we live in the land of the living.

I am the Wind

I am the wind that cometh from the east and from the west from the north and from the south. I am the wind from the corners of the universe where we all need the air to breathe and oxygen to survive, without me what would life be. I am the wind that let you work I am the wind that let you play and I am the wind that let you breathe, so that you can enjoy this life or yet another day. I am the wind that creates the movement of trees, the ripples on the rivers of waters and the roaring of the salty and mighty waves as they come crashing into the endless and winding shores. I am the wind that will let you reminisce the past, I am the wind that gives you peace of mind so that you can meditate on the future of life. I am the wind beneath your wings. I am the wind that you can feel, I am there but you cannot hold me because I am invincible as I travel from place to place with a mind of my own. I am the wind that can make you happy and I am the wind that can make you sad I am the wind that can create havocs in your life as I swirl and move like a tornado over the desert sand, taking with me whatever I can, but without me you are nothing because I am the wind that is beneath your wings.

PERCEPTION OF LIFE

As I walk in the valley that is charred, I see things beyond my beliefs that makes me think and be saddened by the actions of humanity. We are just a human being that was born upon this earth, it is so amazing to see a world that is so wonderful a world that we can share but we care not but a human race that is full of greed as he lives by the passing of each and every day. They say that love conquers hate and good eschewed evil but where is the love that exists in humanity, if there is love, then let us exercise that love and be happy of what we do. We all suffer because of anger and the attitude within ourselves and many times we show no remorse but within our hearts we know what we have done. We can only cry and be sorry but the pain and sorrow that we caused on someone else will still be there for the rest of our lives and in the years to come.

TIME IS THE MASTER

The lives of humanity is just a gift unto us and we know not when the end will come just like the flowers of the morning bloom they are here today but they too shall fade and wither away so as we live we should be thankful and be the best that we can be. Our lives can be better but only if we try and if we fail then we should pick up the pieces and try again because we have to gain that determination and confidence and say to ourselves I can do it. It will not be easy, but what have we to loose when there is nothing to lose and so much to achieve as we gaze into the future that is ahead of us. I have been through the raging fire and I did not get burn and I am willing to take that chance all over again for the betterment of my life and what I want to be in a land where there is birds, bees and wonderful trees as they sway from side to side in the awesome and gentle wind.

I Am the Child

I am the child that was brought into this world without my consent of yes or no. I came as a stranger into a world that is unknown to me with love and respect for humanity. Just like a mother to her children or a father to his fold. I came here as an angel with love to a world of people that I didn't know but as I grow, if I grow? I will know what is there to know and I will know the difference between love and hate and good and evil. I am the child that is innocent that is free from guilt and free of bondage. As a baby I would tie your feet and as I grew to be that man or woman of tomorrow I would tangle your heart. I would make you cry tears of sorrow and sometimes tears of joy, this minute I would break your heart and the next minute I would make you proud, but I am still your child, because a mother's love will never fade away. I am the child that will make choices take up new challenges, create new things so that in the next era we can be the man and woman of tomorrow and will do what it takes so we can be proud of ourselves in the years to come. As the years go by and we grow to be that man and woman of tomorrow, we too shall fade away like the flower of the morning then our seed will grow to be the next child and start their journey from where we left off as we move from one generation into another respectfully.

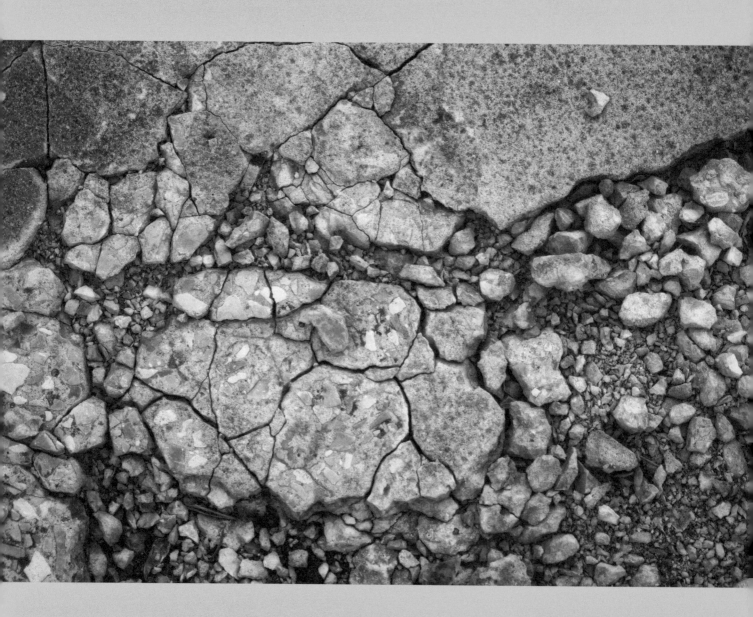

THE CYCLE OF LIFE

I have seen the building of empires and I have seen the falling of empires and all of this is dominion of men and cravings of humanity. What good is it to build an empire when we are creating our own fear of destruction as we live because to every action there is always a reaction. We do things that will conquer the minds of many but we too shall be conquered by someone or something else because what goes around will surely come back around. When we are self-centered bold and powerful, we do things that pleases us but we must remember that we are just human and we are not untouchable but a human being that is born of flesh and bones and a life that is so short that we take it for granted and we know not that what we do today will come back to haunt us tomorrow or in the years to come.

DETERMINATION IN LIFE

Here I sit reminiscing and looking back over my life to see where I was and where I am now, I have to be grateful of where I am and what I am, you too can be proud of yourself of what you are. It will not be easy and it is not a bed that is filled with roses or streets that is made of gold but we manage to lift ourselves from the valley that is dark and gloomy and put ourselves into the light so that we can see more clearly on the brighter side of life. It is all about our determination and dignity that is in us so we thrive to be the best. If we think negative of ourselves then negativity will take hold of us but if we think positive we will move forward and be the best that we can be. Only we can take ourselves into the next dimension of what we want to be and where we want to go.

THE FALLING SNOWFLAKES

As I gaze at the falling of the snowflakes that is moving in every direction as it falls. I see that they are all different in shapes and sizes. It is like a puzzle unto me but this is just another reality in a life that is full of wonders and surprises. As it falls to where it is going by the blowing of the wind it will then accumulate and create a blanket of white and as the warm air pushes forward, it will then be washed away as if nothing was ever there. There and then it reminds me that the reigning of humanity is just for a short time and as we live, we too shall be washed away like the snow and the rain and be lost like a needle in a haystack or just about anything else.

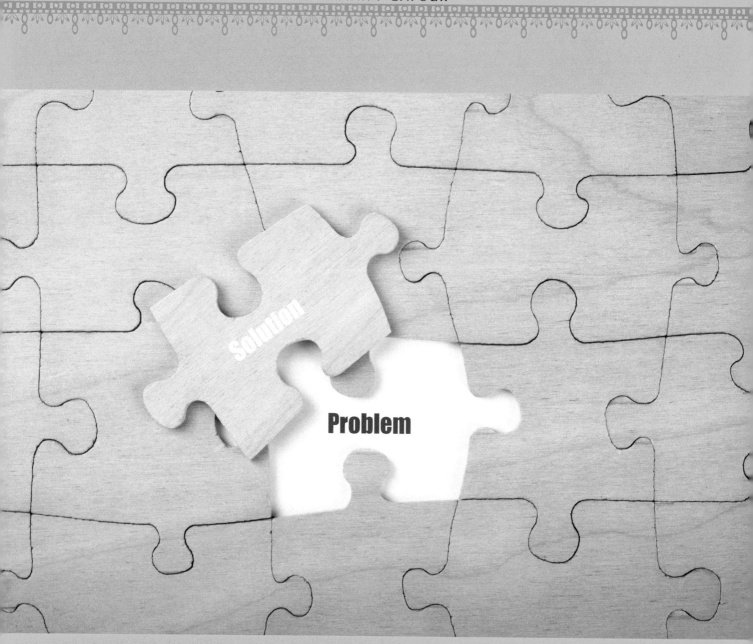

FACING LIFE'S PROBLEMS

I have lived by the passing of each day and as I live my struggles and my torments are greater than before. There and then it is like getting closer to the day that could be the ending of this journey of life. I have seen my life crumbled and disperse in so many ways and there is nothing I can do but live in hope that one day I will free myself from the hate and vile actions of men. I am just another human being that deserves more than what is dished out unto me. My heart cries with pain and sorrow and I ask myself the question, where is the love that is in humanity and why should I live in fear or die for hunger just because we live in a world where love has no meaning and the life of humanity means nothing than just the falling of leaves from the branches of the trees. I have lived a life of misery and fear and I do not know how much more this human being can bear, but if there is a will there should be a way because everything that started will surely come to an end because nothing not one single thing will be here forever.

Trials and Tribulations

The trials and tribulations of life are not just for humanity but for everything that is of this world but only comes in different phases and in different ways and I hope that we all understand and be careful of what we do, because sometimes when we think that we are hurting others, we are hurting our own selves. How can love prevail, when there is no love and no remorse in the hearts of humanity but only hate and discrimination of someone or of something. We cannot see what we are doing that is so wrong and correct ourselves but we can point our fingers at someone else. How can we cast a stone and pretend that we are so innocent. There is an end to everything as justice will be served, but who are we that we should consider someone else when we are thinking about ourselves. We are all living in the same world but in my world I think of no one but myself and my greed that is within me of wanting more and more as I live from one day to the next and when this life is over I will surely pass on that greed to the next generation that is to come and in the years to come.

What is Love?

Love is a treasure that should be cherished forever, but we only love for today and despise by tomorrow. Where is that love from our childhood past is it lost forever, is it the minds of men that are changing and we forget what is love . Love should be a fire that keeps on burning but instead we let the hate that comes between us ruin the love that is in our lives, Is not love stronger than hate? And the roots of a tree stronger than its branches?, should we live in love and be united or should we continue in hate and be divided. Love is vital in a world without love, not just for humanity but for every creature great and small. Show me the love that is in you that I may likewise return it back unto you because life without love is life without hope. When there is love there will be peace and where there is peace there will be unity. Love is a light unto our path and the gift of joy in our lives, love is gracious, love is caring, love is sharing, love is wonderful in all of its splendor and when everything has failed only the gift of love will be strong enough to prevail.

ONLY THE STRONG SURVIVE

It is so amazing what our minds can think but we have to put that amazement to work if we want to achieve our goals in life. We all think of what we want to achieve in our lives but we have to be persistent and put out the best in us so that we can transition our lives into the next dimension. The system of life has many changes as we can see but we have to be grateful as we live and make the best of what we have. Every day we face different obstacles and many different challenges in our daily lives but we have to be humble and smile as we trod in the land of the living because the life we have is just for living and nothing else. This road of life is much more than what we think but we can turn our heartbreak into hope and be the person that we wanted to be and be proud of ourselves for the achievement that we acquire in a world where only the strong survive because of the morality of men with their selfish and crucial mentality as they live by the starting of each day and by the ending thereof.

POWER AND GREED

I have travelled many places during my lifetime and the system of life is all the same, the burning desire of humanity is to achieve more of what he already accomplished, because of greed power and selfishness. There and then I see humanity going deeper and deeper into chaos and destruction as we face another day in our daily lives. Together we can be strong as a race but when we are divided we are subject to our own destruction and failures as we live. Share with me my pain and my sorrow and let us be one and let us build a human foundation that will forever be strong. Suffer me not because I am different from you but let us live in love and share this wonderful life as we live by the passing of each and every day, my mind takes me back into the past, I see humanity drifting more and more into the future where love has no meaning but only the power of men as they existed.

NATURAL DISASTER

As the world shakes with mystery and captured by disaster, the cries of humanity are unbelievable but the forces of nature is far greater than the power of every creature great or small. This is just a reminder unto mankind that we are the dust of the earth and nothing more. These are the signs and wonders of time and it is telling us that we should live in love and harmony, do the best we can as we live in this vast but yet a small world. The craters in life is not just for one but for all, but we ignore the fact that we are the creators of our own mistakes as we live in this wonderful world. The minds of men are troubled by their own creations and they know not what they do. They are dazed and confused as they live in a world of their own, with their mind sets, imaginations and a world of never ending fantasies and will remain that way for the rest of their lives as reality of life will only speak for itself all we have to do is to live by them because reality is the truth in our lives.

THE HEARTACHES OF HUMANITY

You have shuddered me with fear but I will not give up the love that is within me because of you and your selfish ways. What have I done that I should be rejected when you cannot see what you are doing yet you frown from the start of the day to the end of the day. There is no love in your heart or tranquility in your mind, should we continue to live like this until the life of humanity exists no more, or should we examine ourselves and try to change from what we are, so that this world can be a better place for us to live because a life without love is a life of burning heartaches and endless misery. Is it easier to condemn rather than to show love to someone else, then we have to look back into ourselves and see where it is wrong and try to do our best as much as we can. The faces of love that we see on the outside, is much different than the love that is on the inside. You have scarred me with hate and humiliation and I will not condemn you because I will be who I am and what I am and I will take my stand as a human being and be the best I can. I will not let anything hinder me in whatever I do. I will love and love with all my heart and try to live in peace as much as I can because in my world I see a life that is full of love, peace, joy and abundance of happiness

GREATER TRIALS

The pressures of life is unto every man but only comes in different ways and in different phase. The trials of humanity is greater than what he thinks, but he will have to be strong to endure as he lives. The minds of humanity changes like the ticking of the clock and we still cannot be happy of what we have or of what we do. Our minds are troubled and our flesh is weak therefore we doubt ourselves as we live and care not to help someone along the way. I have searched far and wide for happiness and I still cannot find it, maybe it is not there for me or maybe I am thinking too negative and I know not what happiness is. Where is the happiness that I am longing for, am I too blind to see that happiness is right here with me and I know it not, then I know not what is happiness or maybe in my next world I will find happiness. Why should my life be in turmoil as I live, will it be there forever or will it fade away, I do not know, only time will tell as time slips away? I am lost and lonely within myself and I do not know what to do because I am living in fear of myself and everything that is around me. The wind is blowing, the trees are moving, the birds chirping and life is in my body, then I should be happy but instead I am lost like a sheep from the shepherd and I know not where I am or where I should go.

EQUALITY AND LOVE

As I look at the actions of humanity my heart is pounding with fear and desire, the fear is that humanity is in the last days, and on his last journey but our eyes are blinded to everything that we see or maybe we care not but we are falling and it is only because we care for ourselves and not for others. We are selfish and thoughtless as we live and our minds are corrupt and we are darker than the darkness that covers the universe and we will not change because this is what we are and we are only making mistakes that will take us closer to the very end. The desire of humanity come in many different ways and many different phases, we all desire the vanities of life and care less about humanity. Therefore we only think about the gains in our lives but not of life itself. My desire is to see humanity live in peace love and unity, and when we are bonded by unity we can build a strong hold for generations to come and be proud of what we are and of what we do. So let us live a life that we can be proud of with no hesitations in our minds but be happy for the life that we live and when all is said and done we can say to ourselves I have done my best and I am proud of the life that I have lived.

WHAT IS MAN?

What is man? Man was born by the gift of his Creator, yet when he was born he came into this world with nothing. Though he lived, he will have to leave this world as how he came. He will be like the dust that the wind bloweth away in every direction. There and then his image will be lost in space and in time, he will not remember what he has been through or what he has seen because the gift that he once had is lost and I keep asking myself the same question over and over again and I will keep getting the same answers over and over again, What is Man?.

GLITTER IN MY EYES

I've traveled far and wide and I've seen many things that glitter my eyes. Some that are so awesome that I cannot forget it, and some that are not so awesome and I still cannot forget.

There and then I realized when we are traveling this road of life, I found out that the more we live the more we learn and the more we see. Therefore let us do the best that we can and live our lives by the passing of each day and be thankful in every respect for the next minute, the next day is not promised to us by no means or in any respect.

A River Of Dreams

It was on a warm September morning, as the dawning gives way to another day. I decided to walk to the same river that I traveled time and time again, and upon reaching there, I sat on the bank of the river to rest my weary feet.

I then gazed at the water that was running so gentle yet sarcastic in its own ways. There and then I have found peace and tranquility in myself and as I was sitting there I started to wonder what my future will be like, will it be like the rock that gathers no moss or will I live in peace and contentment in the years to come, but I cannot foretell what the future has in store and surely no one can, we will just have to accept what our future has to offer us, as we travel along this mighty endless highway and by the passing of each and every day.

LOVE AND RESPECT

We are just a small fragment of dust that passes through time. We do not know where we are going and surely we do not know what the end will be like. So from the beginning of each day to the end of that day let us look in our hearts and our minds and proudly say to ourselves, I will love and respect every creature great and small for the life that is given to us is just for a very short time. One minute we are here and by the twinkle of an eye we are gone. So let us try to do one good deed in our daily lives and surely we will be happy and proud for what we have done even to the very end, and as we travel from one stage to another respectfully in our own simple ways.

CHANGES IN LIFE

We were born equal from one to another. It is the same genuine and gracious love that brought us here. From the time that was then to the time that we are here now. We tend to change oneself and forget what we are, despising and condemning everything that is around us because it is less than what we are, but we must try to remember there are changes in everyone's life, sometimes it is not for the worst but can also be for the better. Many times we reminisce the past of which, some is good but we have to think of the future that lies ahead and be positive of what we do and how we do it. Because we are only human, and we do make mistakes in our daily lives, because we are not perfect in anyway whatsoever.

FAITH AND FORCES

Time and time again throughout our daily lives we somewhat loose our esteem for ourselves and others it is all because we are losing our faith of what we are and what we can be. Thus our minds start changing from the positive things in our daily lives to those negative thoughts our minds are telling us.

These are the forces that we have to eliminate from our lives and our minds and put them behind us. Therefore when these forces start meddling in our lives we have to stop for just a moment and think of what we are doing and try not to let our own imagination lead us in the wrong direction, in whatever we say or in whatever we do.

ONE DESTINY

I sit here all alone in my own small world, looking at the birds the trees, and gazing into open space wishing and hoping of what my life should be, at that moment in time I was only dreaming of what I wanted to be, but I still do not know what the future holds for me. Then I looked and I saw a puppy walking by without a leash around its neck. It was busy smelling and maybe foraging for food and definitely do not know where she would find a morsel of food to eat to fill its empty stomach or where she would be resting for that night, but still hoping that her dreams would be fulfilled by the time she is ready to rest her weary self. I then realized we both have the same destinies the only difference between us both is that I'm a human being and the other my best friend is a Dog.

THIS PLANET EARTH

How wonderful it is to see the glory of the land and wonders of the deep blue sea. This awesome planet that we share was happily created for us to be as one. For us to enjoy to live in love and oneness by the dawning of each day but because of our diabolical actions against one to another those loving qualities have drifted away and we bring upon ourselves our own damnation. Though often times we blame someone else for our own mistakes but if we could only stop for a moment and look back to what we are doing, we could judge ourselves from a different perspective of what we are and what we can be, there and then we could be the person that we are gifted to be, in our sweet and daily lives.

WHO ARE WE?

We can reminisce the past as we always do, but we have to think of the future and be mindful too. For we think that we are so perfect, so spotless that we often despise others because we are judging them from the outside, but Who Are We? That we should judge others and cannot judge ourselves. Ever so often our thinking can be so enormous and sometimes the same thinking can be so small. Therefore it is good to think positive before we try to engage in any conversations whatsoever.

We all make mistakes and we think that we are the best, but that is just another picture of what we are, in our own ways, and in our own minds.

THE GLOBAL CHANGES

As I travel this road of life, by the passing of each day, I realize the more we live, the more we see the more we learn. It amazes me to see the global changes that are taking place, in time throughout the years that I have lived and I have known this planet called earth. The marching of time waits for no one it slips away so fast, so quickly and sometimes we do not remember what is yesterday and by the blink of an eye another day is gone. There and then it reminds me so much of the changes from our ancestors of the past to all generations of the future. So as we live from one day to the next there will be even greater changes than our eyes can ever behold. So as the night gives way to another day, there will be many surprises in our lives as we live. The lives of many will still be here as the lives of many would be lost. But we have to face whatever realities there are, because we only pass this way just once, only once and we are here no more.

REALITY OF LIFE

If we want to be the person that we want to be in our daily lives, to see our dreams turn into reality to fulfill our daily imagination of what we intend to be, then we have to keep pushing forward. We have to make sacrifices and be loyal to ourselves, because our future depends on what we do. Never doubt yourself by failing just believe in yourself and what you can do and when you have achieved your goals that you have been so longing for, you will be happy and proud to the very end . Therefore we cannot rest until our good is better and our better becomes the very best.

LAND OF THE LIVING

There are so many changes in our daily lives and we have to try to accept them as they face us day by day. But sometimes those changes brought us so much heartaches and so much pain and so often we would say to ourselves what have I done wrong that I should suffer these consequences and tribulations in my daily life but these are trials we have to face as a living being for without those trials we would not be able to tell someone of our past experiences and what we have been through as we live day by day in the land of the living.

BE STRONG

I will do my best and I will never get weary. I will not complain neither will I retreat for I need to make my life more meaningful to advance myself to the next level that I want to be and of what I wanted it to be. Although my struggles seem endless there and then I will be strong. I will proudly hold my head above water and keep moving on because failing is not an option for me. I will not only fail myself but I will fail everyone that is around me so if I fall I will then get up, dust myself off and keep moving on, until my life is more meaningful and what I want it to be in this wonderful world of humanity.

THE BEST IN YOU

Here am I sitting in my own small world. Gazing at the birds, squirrels, and beautiful trees, as they sway to and fro in the cool and gentle wind. My mind races back in time reminding me of what I wanted to be, but to make these dreams a living reality, I will have to put my best foot forward and keep moving onward because the life we have is just for living and nothing more. The system of life has many changes, as we can see, but doubting oneself can only tarnish our integrity, so as we move from one day to the next, let us put out the best in us and keep chasing our dreams as much as we can because when some see the worst in you others will see the best and believe in you.

THIS WONDERFUL WORLD

I have seen a world ahead of me, a world so beautiful only the eyes can see but in my mind lies one small mystery, why? Is there no love or peace among this humanity? If we could just look into ourselves and find where it is wrong. Then our love and peace with humanity will be strong. We commend ourselves on how good we are and easily classify ourselves as the best.

But deep in our hearts it is only a world of make believe and we care not if we mislead or hurt someone as long as we gain their trust in regards to our beliefs. Sometimes unfortunately we are misleading our own selves too because we think so highly of ourselves and no one else so let us make ourselves Humble, Loving and Peaceful as we continue to live and play in this wonderful world by night and splendorous by day where the salty seas roar the four winds blow and the silent and winding rivers flow.

BIRDS TREES AND SEAS

Here I sit in the morning dew, where the grass is green and the flowers are few, my mind is at peace as I listen to the chirping of the birds and the sweet whistling sound of the weeping willow trees. There and then my mind is taking me into a different world a world of great imaginations and fantasy, something that is far beyond anything I have ever imagined. At that moment my imagination is asking me what if you were the only human being in this vast and open world, how happy you will ever be. That I do not know how far you will ever go, again I do not know. I would know the difference between day or night without any doubt whatsoever, but as for me and my imagination I would be lost and tormented as I trod from place to place just to rest my weary self . As I go from place to place, only to find out that I am prohibited by boundaries of some extent. Therefore I would have to accept those boundaries until I can prepare myself to explore and move forward, but those are choices that I have to make within myself if I should go beyond my limits or stay within my boundaries that I am bounded by but as a human being with an open world ahead of me I can only increase my knowledge or stay within my boundaries that I am bounded by and be happy as I live day by day with no one around me, except the salty seas, beautiful trees and the chirping of the birds, as they sing from the dawning of the day to the dusk of the night.

OUR EARTHLY PARADISE

I have travelled far and wide in this wonderful world of humanity. Hoping to find answers to my questions if I can so I will have to learn more of what I see and try to accomplish what I do not know. The further I look is the less I see because my vision is blurred by the distance that is ahead of me. Sometimes we think that the grass is greener on the opposite side but that is just our imagination of how we think. It is very awesome to think positive in our lives, but ever so often we get so negative minded that we lost control of ourselves and we care not of what we say or of what we do so let us be Strong, Wise and Humble as we make it through another day in this magnificent and wonderful world, of our earthly and authentic paradise.

EDGE OF LIFE

I will not judge you neither will I despise you of what you say, or of what you do, but in my mind, I will remember what you are. We are a living being that is born free but because of our negative feelings that is within us we care nothing for the life and well-being of our own humanity. Our lives could be so awesome and wonderful if we could only live with the love that is in our hearts, and think of someone as we think of ourselves. But instead we despise others just by looking at them and we know not that our own reputation will be tarnished as we go from day to day in this awesome life that we have. Yet we know not what the afterlife is all about but we care not what we say or what we do and we know not that we are haters of ourselves. Not knowing that we are living on the edge of life by the passing of each and every day so as we travel on this winding road of life heading towards our own destiny, to our own fate, or maybe a life that is full of fortune and glamour or just disappointments and failures.

LOVE, PEACE AND UNITY

I will make my voice heard without speculation because my mind and my words are free to the extent of my knowledge. In the eyes of you I must be seen but not heard because I am lesser than what you are. You have scorned me because of my integrity and hated me because of my love but who am I that I should hate you back? I am just a human being with blood in my veins and bones within my body so I refrain to sacrifice my integrity, my love and my ability that is within me for something that is of nothing to me. So let us build a foundation of love and harmony instead of building a foundation that is strong and has no meaning. Where there is love and peace there will be happiness and prosperity where there is unity there will be strength and where there is faith there will be hope so let us think more wisely and be creative of what we are doing so that our lives can be more meaningful and prosperous as we share this wonderful world of Birds, Bees and Trees and Rivers that will never cease but a human race that needs greater love from the dawning of the day to the ending thereof.

THE WALK OF LIFE

As I sit here with my mind drifting in so many ways watching the people as they move to and fro in every direction along the streets and avenues, highways and byways, thinking of so many things as they travel from one place to another but still going about their daily routines as usual, seeking what is there to find. These are not just ordinary people but extraordinary people who want to make their lives better in some way whatsoever but unfortunate many got discouraged that they fell by the wayside without hope of seeing their dreams turn to reality as they wish from one day to the next. Life has many surprises than we can ever imagine and we too must remember that patience is the virtue of everything. So let us try to take it day by day and step by step as we walk this walk of life, were time waits for no one, neither can we turn back the hands of time, but do the best we can as we live in this world among the strong and the weak, fear and fearless and some that will never make sacrifices to be a better person as the years go by, or in the years to come.

ABOUT THE AUTHOR

My name is Herman F Gapour and I was born in the Island of Jamaica where I attended school and achieved some of what I have known. During my time in school I wrote short poems for my teachers and my classmates respectfully. It was my dream of coming to the United States of America. And my dream was fulfilled as the years went by. I did not hesitate but took that golden opportunity and put my best foot forward and move to my next destination in my sweet and wonderful life.

My first place of residence was in Washington Seattle. Both my family and I, lived in Seattle for sometimes, then we decided to take up the challenge and go to Queens New York. It wasn't easy but the love and dedication of a family is all we have. Our plan that we have is working in our favor, so I kept writing songs and poems.

My inspiration is the reflection of my surroundings in my daily life, throughout the years I have lived. My love and respect for people is the greatest joy that is in my heart. I will feed into you words of encouragement and love from my heart. I maybe a stranger at first, but a generous and loyal friend to the very end.

Herman F Gapour

Printed in the United States
By Bookmasters